Mourn with those who Mourn

Mourn *with* those who *Mourn*

By

Allison Davis

Published by:

McDougal & Associates
18896 Greenwell Springs Road
Greenwell Springs, LA 70739
www.thepublishedword.com

ISBN 978-1-940461-67-0

Printed on demand in the U.S., the U.K. and Australia
For worldwide distribution

Dedication

I want to dedicate this small reader to everyone facing a challenging season in life. I encourage you to hold your head up and know that a change is coming.

A. Davis

Rejoice with those who rejoice [sharing others' joy], and weep with those who weep [sharing others' grief].

— *Romans 12:15*

Introduction

No words can express the feelings one has when losing a loved one. Whether it's due to separation or the expiration of life on earth, there is still not one flower, card or kind gesture that can cause the very first feeling or reaction to ever go away.

Let me first say that I understand how you may be feeling. After losing my husband, I was very hurt that I would never be able to speak to my best friend again, and I remember telling the Lord how much this bothered me.

I wasn't angry because I understand who the Creator is, but tears would come randomly, and when they began to fall, they became a nearly uncontrollable flood. I cried myself to sleep many nights while talking to the Lord. I know He heard my cry, and I also know that He knows every tear that falls from our eyes and why.

With this bit of background on my story, I'm here to let you know today that I deeply understand the season you're in and want to assure you that help is never far away.

— Allison Davis

What Is Grief?

The word **grief** comes from a Latin term **gravare**, which means "to make heavy." In the English language **grief** is defined as "deep sadness or sorrow over the sudden loss of someone or something to which a bond or affection has been formed." Grief is a natural emotional response to loss, but it certainly is "heavy."

What Does God's Word Say about Grief?

Psalm 30:5 tells us that **"weeping may endure for a night, but a shout of joy comes in the morning."** This lets us know that there will be an end to mourning. Grief has its purpose, but it also has its limits. That is very good news indeed.

Taking Life One Day at a Time

After shedding some light on how you feel during this season and why you're feeling this way, it is now time to take things one day at a time. The best way to do this to get connected and stay connected with a group of strong, praying believers in Christ. This is a great way to ensure that you won't get stuck in the spirit of grieving and grieve too long.

Yes, grieving is a spirit, and it affects us in many different ways.

I actually didn't discover this until the loss of my loved one. The body of believers that surrounded me encouraged me, loved me and helped lift me up in that dark period.

We can only live one day at a time, and that's how God allows us to live— one day at a time. Knowing that God has created a family for us allows us to get through this troubling period easier. Eventually, the phone calls will stop and the flowers will stop coming, but God's love is eternal, and His people know how to express that love.

After the loss of my husband, I had arrived at a place in my life where

I felt as if I had been pushed into a corner and forced to remain silent. This season did not last long because I cried out to God. I was advised to see a counselor. This allowed me to speak out about the feelings I was experiencing and get relief.

Be careful not to push God's people away in your time of need. We need to speak out about how we feel and allow ourselves time to go through the healing process, but it's more than that. Galatians 6:2 tells us that the whole Body of Christian believers has been given the ability to **Mourn with Those Who Mourn.** The love that

God has placed inside of the hearts of every believer is available to you, if you will just choose to accept it.

Some of us, however, don't believe we need help ... until someone brings it to our attention. Be informed that the emotional roller-coaster you have been on will stop, but only when you finally reach out and get help.

Doing a Self-Check

On the next page you will find a check list that can help you identify and confront the way you feel about your loss or your separation from a loved one. These questions will help you get through the beginning stages of this season in your life. Answer them honestly and openly and believe God to help you with what you find:

	<u>Yes</u>	<u>No</u>

Are you feeling anger of some sort? _ _

If so, why?

Are you feeling some regret? _ _

If so, why?

Are you feeling hurt? _ _

If so, why?

Are you feeling guilt? _ _

If so, why?

Are you feeling sadness? _ _

If so, why?

This "if-so-why" question can help you carefully examine your feelings about the loss or separation you have suffered. Then, allow me to express the truth that none of these feelings will go away without you first acknowledging them and giving them to God. There's no anger, regret, hurt feelings or sorrow that can be expressed to your loved one after their passing. This is the reason God's Word tells us in James 5:16, **"confess your sins to one another ... , and pray for one another, that you may be healed and restored."** For this reason, we must not lose any time before making things right with others, while they are still here with us. After they are gone, it's too late.

I recently took this self-check test just to be sure I didn't have any unresolved issues myself. I must admit that I do still feel sad at times. I truly miss talking with my husband and constantly letting him know how much I loved him. If, for some reason, you did not make things right between yourself and your loved one before their passing, then allow me to assure you that healing is still available for you. You cannot seek forgiveness from them, but God can still heal your broken heart.

Are You Angry?

Were you (or are you still) angry with someone who has passed away? If so, then you must not live in that anger any longer. You must release all your anger to God and allow Him to heal you from any offense or affliction that was caused by the person who passed.

Do You Have Regrets?

Are you going through your mind and finding something that you regret doing or even not doing to or for a loved one who is now passed away? Again, there's no way for you to apologize to them, but God can ease those feelings and give you peace. You must repent and ask God for forgiveness and then take it a step further, by forgiving yourself. This will release you from the past and allow you to move toward your future.

Do You Feel Hurt?

Have you been hurt by something that was said or done to you by the person who passed away? There's no way they can apologize for what they may have done wrong. So, in this case, you must simply stop waiting for an apology.

In most cases the people who hurt us don't apologize anyway, but the way to heal from this is to lay it on the altar before God. Allow Him to heal your wounds and mend your heart.

Are You Feeling Guilty?

Are you feeling guilty because you know you have not been the best person to a loved one who has passed away? Did you lead them wrong in some way? There's forgiveness at the cross for you as well. Jesus paid the price and made the ultimate sacrifice because of our sin nature.

You must repent, turn away from your sin and follow Christ (see Luke 13:3). Although we cannot go back in time, Jesus has already fixed it.

Are You Feeling Sad?

Are you sad due to the loss of a loved one or a separation? I have learned that it's okay to cry, and it doesn't really matter who's watching. I remember being at the grocery store one day, and tears overtook me. I began to pray and continued my shopping. What matters most is that you are allowing yourself to express outwardly what you are feeling after losing someone.

Don't worry about what others may think.

But being sad also has its limits. Remember, God's Word says **"joy comes in the morning."** So don't just cry and then sit alone and be lonely. Have hope that joy is coming your way, and then choose to be joyful in your new situation.

No Matter What You Are Feeling

No matter what you are feeing, allow me to encourage you that there's nothing that catches God by surprise. He knew that this season of your life would come. His Word also reminds us that He knew us before we were ever formed in our mother's womb.

There is nothing that you cannot go to God in prayer about. If suffering a loss or separation of a loved one is hurting you, then you should open up and let God know it. Tell Him, "Lord, this hurts!" Then, after going to the Father, having faith and believing in Christ, you must allow Him to heal all your hurts and replace them with His joy.

It's Time to Live

Surely there is still someone depending on you to live your life skillfully. You can't allow yourself to get lost in emotion and stuck in a rut forever. At some point in time, you have to dry your face and decide to live. The purpose of your existence is counting on you to live your life and maximize your full potential here on earth.

You may not be aware of it, but the whole world is grieving. It's something we all go through in life. This does not stop the move of God at all, and it should not stop you. Others are counting on you to get to where you need to be in life so that you can encourage them or lift them up, even lend them a hand. So, you see, grieving does have its limits because there's a time to weep and a time to rejoice.

Every believer should understand what it means to be absent from the body. Paul wrote to the Corinthians: **"to be absent from the body and to be at home with the Lord"** (2 Corinthians 5:8). So, have hope that your loved one who has passed away is present with the Lord.

For those who are grieving the separation from a loved one, be certain not to leave anyone wounded. Clear your conscience and allow the prisoners in your heart and mind to be set free. Forgive those who have afflicted or wounded you, for this is the only way you can live a victorious life, one filled with freedom.

We have no right to control other people, for this is considered to be witchcraft (trying to control the mind of another). So, if someone decides to walk out of your life, you should let them go freely. Then continue walking in love and joy, knowing that God cares for you.

In Conclusion

I want to leave you with a scripture to hold on to. The words of this passage were the first thing the Lord spoke to me after I had lost my husband:

Though he slay me, yet will I trust him: but I will maintain mine own ways before him.   Job 13:15, KJV

This allows me to remind myself that no matter what trials I may face and how bad it may hurt, I will always trust in the Lord and He will surely see me through.

Author Contact Page

If this book has been a blessing,
you may contact the author directly
in the following ways:

Allison Davis
729 N. Joe Wilson Road
Cedar Hill, TX 75104

chinyeres.llc@gmail.com